Applied Psychology

Volume 8

MIND

MECHANISM

Being the Eighth of a Series of Twelve Volumes on the Applications of Psychology to the Problems of Personal and Business Efficiency

BY

WARREN HILTON, A.B., L.L.B.

FOUNDER OF THE SOCIETY OF APPLIED PSYCHOLOGY

ISSUED UNDER THE AUSPICES OF
THE LITERARY DIGEST
FOR
NEW YORK AND LONDON
1919

COPYRIGHT 1914
BY THE APPLIED PSYCHOLOGY PRES5
SAN FRANCISCO

ISBN-13:
978-1499585933

ISBN-10:
1499585934

CONTENTS

Chapter V. page 47
FOUR ADDITIONAL LAWS OF SUCCESS-ACHIEVEMENT

FUNDAMENTAL LAWS OF ACHIEVEMENT

Mind Mechanism

MAN'S DYNAMIC POWER

Chapter I

MAN'S DYNAMIC POWER

A DAWNING CONCEPT

IN PRECEDING volumes we have outlined the mental processes and presented to you some new and interesting mind facts and phases. The time has come now for us to marshal our facts, to indicate the scientific method of handling them, and to show you how to make use of them in a practical way.

Your mental operations determine the course of your career. To intelligently direct them you must have a scientific conception of your mind as a whole, one that you can use in clearing the way to health, success and happiness.

THE TWENTIETH CENTURY "NEW WORLD"

The existence of any mental activities outside of consciousness would have been, and in fact was, ridiculed fifty, even twenty-five, years ago. It is only within the last few years that through investigation of hypnotic and other abnormal mental phenomena scientific men have discovered a mental world that was previously unknown.

This discovery offers possibilities greater than any that could possibly result from discoveries in the world of matter. This new-found depth to the spiritual side of man reveals energies and powers as relatively great when compared with the "mind" of fifty years ago as the applied electricity of today surpasses in importance the lightning that Franklin drew from the clouds.

Since this discovery there has been an astonishing upspringing of religious, metaphysical and psychological cults. Vast numbers of men and women are enlisted in them. People in all walks of life are interested in their preachments. Newspapers and magazines abound in articles concerning them.

THE FETISH OF THE "NEW THOUGHT"

There is truth in all these cults. Yet all are but transitory phases of a dawning conception of the dynamic power of man.

Nearly all these "psychic" movements center about the idea that there is a "subconscious mind," a distinct entity, having no connection with the mind of consciousness, except as the latter may be a source of information to the "subconscious mind" as to what goes on in the external world.

The "subconscious mind" is the fad of the hour. It is the chief topic of discussion in religious circles, health resorts and women's clubs. It is the fetich of the "New Thought." It is employed by the unlettered with as much easy assurance as by the scientific.

There are those who assert that as a separate mind it reasons and reaches conclusions by processes different from any with which we are acquainted.

THE CLAMOR OF TRANSITION

Some there are who address it familiarly as a distinct personality. Others look upon it as the intelligence that directs the operation of bodily functions on the one hand, while at the same time it is identical in substance with the most sacred treasures of religious belief.

For some it is the source of every expression of true genius. With others it is the medium through which speak the spirits of the mighty dead.

And amid all this clamor of enthusiasm and acclaim bold-voiced scientists of high repute scoffingly assert that as to this alleged separate "sub conscious mind" its story "may be told in three words: 'There is none.'"

THE CONCEPTUAL MODELS OF SCIENCE

Chapter II

THE CONCEPTUAL MODELS OF SCIENCE

TEST OF THE TRULY SCIENTIFIC

IT WOULD be folly for you to approach this subject, about which there exists such widespread confusion of thought, without a prior study of basic principles. You cannot discriminate intelligently among these different conclusions without first formulating in your own mind the rules by which you are to be guided in arriving at a decision.

You must put every theory of the subconscious, or, in more scientific language, every conception of the sub conscious, to the test of conformity with the methods of science. To do this you must first frame your test.

It is universally recognized that no theory or conception can be regarded as truly scientific or justifiable unless it contains certain well-defined elements.

The thing to do now, therefore, is to find out what elements must enter into a conception of the subconscious before that conception can be regarded as truly scientific.

You can then put these elements together into a conceptual model, and by this model as a standard of truth you may test the various theories of the sub conscious.

SCIENTIFIC SYMBOLISM

The words "science" and "scientific" are commonly regarded as having a much more restricted meaning than rightfully belongs to them. Men talk of "the sciences," having in mind only mathematics, chemistry, physics, those sciences which have to do with the phenomena of matter.

As a matter of fact, any branch of classified human knowledge is a science, the term being just as applicable to one department of the classified facts of human experience as to another. Mathematics is no more truly scientific than history. The historian, if he pursues his researches in a scientific manner, is bound by the same rules as is the mathematician.

CLASSIFICATIONS AND GENERALIZATIONS

That which distinguishes science on the one hand from speculation, from religious philosophy on the other, is not the nature of its facts, but the method used in their investigation.

Whatever the problem may be, whether it arises in the study of chemistry or astronomy or language or history, whether it relates to mind or matter, actual experience must furnish the only elements that may scientifically be employed in its solution.

Science deals solely with the facts of human experience. These facts it submits to the two basic processes of Classification and Generalization.

The scientist classifies all the facts relating to his problem into sequences. That is to say, he groups together as evidence all of the known instances in which one event, "B," follows upon another, "A." From such a collection Generalizations of sequences, the investigator deduces a general principle.

And if this general principle is properly accredited — that is to say, if in a vast number of instances "B" invariably follows upon "A," and the utmost research has failed to reveal a single instance in which "B" does not follow upon "A" —

then this principle is recognized as a Scientific Law.

Now, these generalizations or laws are not expressed in terms of actual things. They contain no reference to physical realities that anyone ever actually heard or felt or saw.

They are written in the broadest form possible.

"ARTICLES" AND "ELECTRONS"

They are written in symbolic terms, representing the essential character of things — that is to say, in terms not of things, but of qualities of things. The terms in which such laws are expressed stand for purely abstract conceptions. Take, for example, the law of gravity, "any particle attracts any other particle, "a" particle" being defined as an infinitely small portion of matter. Or consider the modern scientific theory that every atom is composed of "electrons," each revolving in its own tiny orbit about a central point. Now, Newton, who framed the law of gravity, never saw a "particle," nor has any man ever seen or otherwise had sensory knowledge of an "electron." The "electron" and "particle" are, in other words, Imaginary things, abstract ideas, theoretical conclusions, arrived at by reducing sensory experiences to their essential qualities.

WEIGHTLESS, FRICTIONLESS ETHER

The ether, of whose "waves" and "vibrations" physics has so much to say, is of precisely similar character. In a way, it actually does violence to all our experiential knowledge of physical things, for it is imagined as having neither weight nor friction.

So, too, the "points" and "lines" of geometry are imagined as being without substance and as occupying no space.

In other words, the "particle," the "ether," the "line," the "point," are none of them concrete realities.

Like the letters of algebra, they are merely symbolic terms employed by scientist in the solution of his problem. They are physical facts reduced to their theoretical or conceptual essence and are therefore technically known as concepts.

PREDICTING FUTURE EVENTS

The value of the whole system lies in the fact that by it we are enabled to deduce from the facts of experience laws of such general application that we may apply them to the widest possible variety of appropriate facts, and in this way predict future events.

Now, what may constitute the essence of a given fact of experience depends altogether upon the point of view of the investigator. It depends upon the purpose or subject of the investigation.

WHAT EACH MAN SEES

The essential factor for one may be of no consequence to another. The petal of a rose to a geometrician is an irregular solid bounded by curved surfaces. To the chemist it is an aggregate of atoms. To neither is it a living thing of fragrant beauty.

In other words, the same fact may be differently conceived according to the point of view. Each investigator sees that element only which is pertinent to his own scientific aim. The concept of one may be just as valuable as the concept of another. Each is of value only in its own field of research.

In an earlier volume we pointed out that all our knowledge comes to us through the senses. The senses are our only means of communication with the outer world. All experience is sensory experience. All the facts of experience are in the last analysis merely sense impressions.

WHAT SCIENCE WORKS WITH

Sense impressions are the sole material of modern science. No scientific man, whatever his subject, considers that he is dealing with "things in themselves." He is perfectly aware that sense-impressions are the only realities, the only things of which he has or can have direct knowledge, and that the world for him as for everyone else is a mental world.

What, then, do scientists, psychologists and physicists mean when they speak of material or physical things as distinguished from mental, when they distinguish between mind and matter?

TERM CONFUSION

The answer is this: The psychologist and the physicist have entirely different scientific conceptions. They look at the world from two different points of view.

Each selects from his facts those elements and adopts those conceptions that are suited to his needs. The physicist is writing a story of the world of experience in terms of motion and structure. The psychologist is writing the story of the world of experience in terms of ideas, emotions and impulses.

Consequently, when you come to devise mental concepts and enunciate mental laws, you must confine yourself to mental terms. You must not invade, for example, the field of physiology. You must not frame your laws in terms drawn from the dissecting-room. You must not try to get down to the essential qualities of brain and nerve tissue.

When you find that the awakening of an idea in memory brings with it certain muscular activities, you must conceive them as resulting not from the potential physical energy in the nucleus of a brain cell, but from the potential mental energy of an idea.

THE MENTAL SUB-CELLAR

Chapter III
THE MENTAL SUB-CELLAR

BRAIN-FACTS AND MIND-FACTS

WITH these distinctions clearly in mind, you are in a position to examine in the light of first principles the various theories or conceptions of the subconscious.

In the midst of all the diversity of opinion among scientific men and reputable lay writers, four theories may be said to predominate. Let us briefly summarize these.

1. Some psychologists regard all mental phenomena as nothing more nor less than manifestations of brain activity. This is the point of view of "descriptive psychologists." With them, subconscious activities are but the outward expression of "unconscious cerebration" — that is to say, brain action, brain-cell activities, of which we are unconscious.

Now, with due respect to these distinguished authorities, you, as a student of the mind, must certainly deal with the facts of anesthesia in hysterical persons, the facts of "dissociated personalities," the facts of automatic bodily operations, as expressions of mind activity. They may be immediately caused by brain- or nerve-cell activity. But brain- or nerve-cell activity may in turn have been produced by mind action.

In any event, you are investigating Mixing the mind, not the body, and to look upon bodily activities as the result of brain action is to jump from one mode of conceiving things to the other. It is to mix mental and physiological conceptual terms in a manner incompatible with scientific methods.

Nerve fibers cannot be scientifically conceived as forming a connection between two ideas.

You are after practical results.

Your theory of the mind and sub consciousness must explain mental phenomena and enable you to frame mental laws for your future guidance.

THE "FRINGE" OF CONSCIOUSNESS

Your theory of the subconscious must be based upon purely mental conceptions. It must be constructed wholly out of terms of mind. Only in this way will you be able to so express the laws of mind and apply them in your daily life as to secure the highest degree of, efficiency in your mental operations and employ to the fullest extent your mental energies.

2. The term "subconscious" is used' by some to define that portion of the field of consciousness which at any moment lies just outside the focus of the attention. By them the subconscious is conceived as an area of restricted attention. To them sub consciousness means merely the marginal horizon or "fringe" of consciousness. And, in this connection, the prefix "sub" implies merely the limited awareness that we have for these facts of consciousness out of the corner of the mind's eye. It is obvious that used in this way the term "subconscious" represents no scientific conception whatever. It is simply a term used to describe certain parts of the field of consciousness, to designate certain facts of experience as but dimly recognized in consciousness as compared with certain other facts.

"SPLIT-OFF" IDEAS

3. The third use of the term "subconscious" is that in which it is employed chiefly by medical men and students of the psychology of the abnormal. To these men subconscious ideas are ideas which have been dissociated or "split off" from the waking or, as they say, "normal" consciousness, "split off" from the main personal consciousness to such a degree that the owner in his normal state is unaware of their existence.

These dissociated ideas may consist merely of isolated and lost sensations, as in the anesthesia of hysterical patients, or they may be assembled into aggregate and organized groups of sensations. In the latter case they form a consciousness that exists simultaneously with the primary consciousness, and we have the so-called "double" or "multiple" personality.

Now, such a person in his state of primary consciousness has no immediate knowledge of his secondary consciousness, and, vice versa, his secondary consciousness has no immediate knowledge of the existence of the primary consciousness. If either learns of the existence of the other, it is by deduction from appearances or from information which is gathered from other persons.

A CONCEPTION THAT FALLS SHORT

Meanwhile, the observer, the medical psychologist, deduces the existence of this subconscious state from its outward manifestations, just as he deduces the existence of ordinary consciousness in other persons, not directly, but by inference from their physical manifestations and his own sense-perception of them.

For the student of the mind, then, this secondary consciousness, so far as its essential nature is concerned, is not in any respect different from the ordinary consciousness.

If Professor Janet or Dr. Prince engages in conversation with an individual whose hand, at the same moment and without the knowledge of his primary consciousness, writes answers to the questions of a third person whispered in his ear, then Professor Janet or Dr. Prince will speak of this automatic writing as a manifestation of sub consciousness just as he would speak of the patient's conversation as a manifestation of consciousness.

No attempt is made to reason back of the manifestation and determine how it came about. These men merely recognize the coexistence of the conscious and what they call the subconscious. They do not pretend to offer a scientific conception amounting to an explanation. In the words of Dr. Janet, "it is a simple clinical observation of a common character which these phenomena present.

More than this, the opinion is steadily gaining ground among investigators of this type that the subconscious actually has no part in these manifestations of abnormal mental action. There is a general tendency among them to adopt the suggestion of Dr. Prince and describe such dissociated ideas, organized or disorganized, as "co-conscious," instead of "subconscious."

Now, to limit the term subconscious to abnormal dissociations of ideas of the character we have referred to, falls far short of your requirements. It offers no theory of the mind that you can employ in the practical affairs of your life.

"DUAL MINDS"

These physicians are concerned only with the manifestations of mental abnormalities and diseased minds. They are not trying to solve the mystery of the healthy normal mind. In the luxuriant garden of the mind they observe only the evidences of decay.

4. The fourth use of the word "subconscious" is an elaboration and expansion of the third. This fourth meaning of the term- is that in which it is employed by the great majority of lay writers.

These writers proclaim the existence of two distinct "minds." One of these "minds," the objective, is the mind of sense-impressions, the mind of consciousness, the mind that receives all messages from the outer world and in turn conducts all our immediate activities in relation to it. The other of these "minds" is the subjective. It is entirely outside of consciousness. It has no direct communication with the outer world. We are not directly aware of its existence. It is for each man his individual segment of the Spirit of God.

IDEALISTIC SPECULATION

This last theory, that of the lay writers, is distinctly metaphysical and appeals strongly to the imagination. It is idealistic and fascinating. But it is obvious that the term "sub consciousness" is here taken altogether outside the domain of science and inscribed in the dictionary of religious and speculative philosophy.

PREVAILING CONCEPTIONS OF THE "SUBCONSCIOUS"

Summarizing these different views, we find :

1. That the term "subconscious" is employed by different writers to identify phenomena belonging to entirely different fields of thought.

2. That although these observed facts are strictly mental phenomena, and, so far as you are concerned, should be viewed from the standpoint of the psychologist, many authorities so unfortunately confuse them with physiological material that they seem to make no distinction between mind and brain, and that mind -facts and brain -facts seem to be for them interchangeable terms.

3. That through the writings of laymen the popular mind has become befuddled with vague and speculative explanations of the facts, explanations that may actually be true, but are in the Prevailing very nature of things incapable of proof and are utterly out of place in a scientific study of the subject. They are excursions into the dream forest of mysticism, occultism and religion.

4. That of the two theories of the subconscious that may properly be classed as scientific, one defines it as "the fringe of consciousness," the other defines it as a concurrent consciousness, a "co-consciousness," made up of active but

dissociated elements of the main or primary consciousness.

You must agree with us that these definitions are narrow and inadequate. You require a scientific conception of the subconscious that shall view the subject in all its phases, shall make broad generalizations possible, and shall thus realize for the mind its full possibilities of usefulness in all the relations of men.

Every one of the theories of the subconscious that we have outlined falls before one or the other of two objections.

The speculative and metaphysical theory falls before the objection that it is unscientific. The conception of the physicians and the men of scientific repute falls before the objection that it is of limited practical value.

Now, a scientific conception of the subconscious, which shall be at the same time sufficiently broad for general practical use, will not only show you how to cure mental diseases or any other sort of functional diseases, but will also enable you to solve every problem in which mental operations are a factor.

CONCEPT THE BUSINESSMAN NEEDS

Mental operations are not only a factor, but they are the one and important factor in every phase of a man's career. Consequently you must have a conception of the subconscious that you can use like an algebraic formula in meeting your daily needs, hopes and responsibilities.

The sort of conception of the subconscious that you require must be justifiable from the standpoint of science and must at the same time be sufficiently comprehensive to account for all forms of mental activity outside of consciousness. What you want is a scientific explanation of normal mental processes as well as a scientific explanation of abnormal mental processes.

And, to merit the term "scientific," your conception must conform to the three requirements of every scientific concept: First, it must he expressed in terms that represent the reduction of facts to their essential properties; second, it must be expressed wholly in mental as distinguished from physiological terms, and, third, it must explain all the facts in the sense that no facts can be found to which the explanation could not logically be made to apply.

AN INVENTION FOR DEVELOPING POWER

Chapter IV

AN INVENTION FOR DEVELOPING POWER

FUNDAMENTAL CONCLUSIONS

IN THE volumes that preceded this study of the subconscious we did something more than merely catalogue facts. We put forward tentatively a number of conclusions embodying some of the elements of the subconscious. What we have to do now is to marshal, systematize and arrange these conclusions and such others as we may require into workable form for everyday use. Consequently we shall first set forth briefly the conclusions arrived at in former lessons and then tell you just what the subconscious is.

First — Every human being has but one mind. Its phases and elements are many.

Second — Every human body is the abode not only of the consciousness that perceives and reacts to sense-impressions, but also of countless cellular intelligences, each of which instinctively utilizes ways and means for the performance of its special function and the reproduction of its kind. These cell intelligences under a supervisory control embodied in the sympathetic nerve system carry on without our knowledge or volition — that is to say subconsciously — the vital functions of the body.

Third — All sensory experiences whether perceived or not, whether capable of voluntary recall or not, are somehow and somewhere mentally preserved.

Fourth — Every idea thus stored in sub consciousness possesses an inherent latent energy tending to produce some particular form of muscular activity.

Fifth — Whether we are conscious or unconscious, a certain element of the mind, which we may call "attention", is ever vigilantly awake and bars from consciousness all incoming sense-impressions and all suggested memories excepting those which it has been trained to select and admit.

Sixth — The attention is subject to control by the will.

A SCIENTIFIC CONCEPT
OF PRACTICAL UTILITY

We have stated these propositions again in order to refresh your memory concerning them. It might be well for you briefly to review the previous books at this point, to trace again the course of reasoning by which these various conclusions were arrived at. This is suggested that they may be the more firmly fixed in your mind as logical deductions from the facts.

We submit now a conception of the subconscious that fills all the requirements of practical usefulness and of conformity with scientific methods. Sub consciousness is all there is of the individual mind not embraced in the passing momentary consciousness. As such, it includes all the primary instincts with which man comes into the world, as such, it is the sum total all his individual cellular intelligences. It is that department of mind which directs the nourishment and repair of the body and automatically operates the vital functions. It is the repository in which are retained all sensory experiences, conscious or unconscious, remembered or forgotten.

Sub consciousness is a vast reservoir, of ideas, emotions and motor impulses, from which is drawn the greater part of the elements of which consciousness is composed, for consciousness consists in part of present sensory experiences, but far the greater part of its contents is made up of "thoughts" drawn from the warehouse of the past.

The ideas, emotions and motor impulses thus retained in sub consciousness are grouped together and classified for purposes of ready reference by the associative processes of the mind into "groups" and "complexes."

All ideas stored in sub consciousness possess a latent or potential energy which becomes kinetic or circulating energy when they are drawn actively into the changing momentary consciousness. This energy is an impulse to some form of muscular activity, so that every idea in sub consciousness has associated with it the impellent energy necessary to produce a particular muscular motion.

Every idea stored in sub consciousness has associated with it not only an impellent energy, but also an emotional quality appropriate to the inherent character of the idea.

If mental images in which you are yourself triumphant, victorious, successful, are drawn into your consciousness, they tend to outwardly manifest themselves in such bodily activity as may be appropriate to your part in the picture and to beget within you at the same time feelings of health, invigoration, capability and power.

Conversely, if complexes or ideas constituting mental pictures of misfortune, disease and death become active in your consciousness, they bring with them impulses that tend to depress the action of your heart and other vital organs of your body and to restrain all bodily activity, while at the same time they weigh you down with feelings of self-abasement, dejection and melancholy.

The extent of the influence of any idea or group of ideas or complex of associated mental elements, once it becomes active in consciousness, depends upon the relation in which it stands to the other elements of consciousness.

If there are at the same time present in your consciousness one or more conflicting ideas or groups of ideas, the given idea will be but faintly portrayed to your mind's eye. Its emotional qualities will touch you but lightly, and its impulses to muscular activity will be more or less restrained.

If, on the other hand, the given idea holds undisputed sway in your consciousness, if no conflicting or inhibitory ideas and impulses are simultaneously present, then the mental picture is painted with bold strokes and clear perspective, with high lights and deep shadows. It stands forth as an assured reality, and you have the phenomenon commonly called "belief."

For "faith" or "belief" is nothing more nor less than the presence of an idea in consciousness freed from the restraints of contrary thoughts.

This is the subconscious as you must conceive it and the nature of the tie that binds it to the personal consciousness.

Our course of reasoning has been true and our assumptions have been well and logically made, and you will, find that all future happenings in your actual experience will accord with the principles we have deduced.

THE SEQUENCE OF SCIENCE

We want you to observe particularly that we have here the sequence that characterizes all scientific methods: first, the collection and classification of facts, as in our collection and marshaling of subconscious mental activities in this Course; secondly, the invention of a conception to explain these facts.

All laws of physical science have been evolved in just this way. Kepler collected data concerning the changing positions of the planets and demonstrated that they moved in elliptical orbits around the sun. Newton subsequently brought forward the law of gravity with the conception of an un- seen force as an explanation of Kepler's facts and as a means for foretelling the future action of the planets and other masses of matter.

ULTIMATE MENTAL ELEMENTS

Our conception of the subconscious not only accounts for the existence of all known mental phenomena, but it is expressed in terms of ultimate and abstract elements along scientific lines. With these elements we have already framed, and will still further frame, laws intended to sum up past mental experience and enable us to predict the outcome of any future mental action.

How different this conception from the sub consciousness of the students of abnormal psychology! Applying our principles to their facts, we conclude that while normally consciousness is a unit, it may at times, through an abnormal or deranged functioning of attention or dissociation, become split up into two or more coexisting consciousnesses of different composition. Each of these consciousnesses may be systematically organized, but one of them is usually associated with a more profound system of memory than the other, and is therefore called the primary consciousness. In this way are brought about those abnormal manifestations ranging from mere loss of feeling in some part of the body to dissociated "personalities."

You can now see that our conception of the subconscious is very different from any of the prevailing doctrines of this phase of mental activity as we have outlined them. It is a conception that you have set for yourself.

SEEING A SUBCONSCIOUS COMPLEX

It is wholly a psychical as distinguished from a physiological conception. It takes into account the whole array of subconscious phenomena land reduces them to elementary terms.

In this conception you rise above the level of mere facts to the plane of pure abstractions. Have you ever seen or heard or felt a "subconscious complex"? Have you ever seen or heard or felt or in any way been conscious of a system of associated ideas, emotions and impulses which were not at the time in consciousness? The very proposition is absurdly self-contradictory.

But neither has any man ever seen an "electron" nor the infinitely small "particle" of matter, nor had sensory experience of the weightless, frictionless ether. If the subconscious is something that it would be impossible for anyone to perceive through the medium of the senses, so is the infinitely small "particle" of matter something that it would be impossible for anyone to perceive through the senses.

Do not suppose for a moment that the acceptance of this theory of the mind precludes any particular form of religious belief. On the contrary, it is in perfect harmony with the most highly idealized conception of the spiritual quality of man.

ORIGIN OF THE THOUGHT STREAM

It is the author's individual belief that there is an Inner Spirit more directly at one with the Deity than any mere mental function. It may even be origin of the that the subconscious phases of the stream mind bring us into a more intimate communion with God than any phase of consciousness, and that sub consciousness is the actual instrument of communication between the Infinite and man. It may be that in sleep and in moments of profound reflectiveness, before the life of consciousness intervenes, the Divine Father is nearest to his children. It may be that this stream of thought that flows upward through us from sub consciousness into consciousness, may find its origin in the Divine Mind and Heart. Who can tell? We know not. These things may; be true, but they cannot be verified. They cannot be put to the acid test of the reason. And, as you learned in an earlier book, it is unnecessary to the scientific pursuit of self-conscious ends that we should determine "first" causes.

FOUR ADDITIONAL LAWS OF SUCCESS-ACHIEVEMENT

Chapter V

FOUR ADDITIONAL LAWS OF SUCCESS-ACHIEVEMENT

FUNDAMENTAL LAWS OF ACHIEVEMENT

IT IS well that you should mark again at this time our three original fundamental principles of Success - Achievement, to which we shall here add certain other principles that you must now regard as established.

I. All human achievement comes about through some form of bodily activity.

II. All bodily activity is caused, controlled and directed by the mind.

III. The mind is therefore the instrument that we must employ in the accomplishment of any purpose.

IV. You have but one mind, but it is a mind with phases of consciousness and phases of sub consciousness.

V. Your consciousness is made up in part of present sensory experiences and in part of complexes drawn from sub consciousness.

VI. Your sub consciousness is a vast mental reservoir of classified complexes made up of ideas, emotions and motor impulses.

VII. The presence of any idea in your consciousness tends simultaneously to produce an associated "feeling" and to impel you to certain appropriate muscular activities.

You now have a conception of the human mind on the order of the conceptions of physical science.

We shall show you how to make this conception of as great practical value in harnessing the forces of your own mind as any other scientific conception has been in harnessing the forces of the physical world.

The trained business mind is forever storing in its subconscious stronghold facts that will be needed and lessons to be drawn from them. It has its facts, its principles, its details of commercial transactions at instant command. It is the unfailing source of Energy, Courage, Confidence, Enthusiasm and Practical Ability. You who are beset with doubts and perplexities, with wasteful passions and unmanly fears, must train this deeper mind to set you free and to reveal greater and richer opportunities for achievement.